FUNK LORE

AMIRI BARAKA

New Poems (1984–1995)

Edited by Paul Vangelisti

LITTORAL BOOKS
LOS ANGELES · 1996

© Amiri Baraka 1996
All rights reserved

Cover Art by Amiri Baraka
Typography by Guy Bennett

ISBN 1-55713-296-8

Contents

- 9   J. said, "Our whole universe is generated by a rhythm"
- 11   Masked Angel Costume: The Sayings of Mantan Moreland
- 15   Sounding
- 20   Brother Okot
- 22   Forensic Report
- 25   Why It's Quiet in Some Churches
- 27   Sin Soars!
- 37   Ode to the Creature
- 39   X
- 40   I Am
- 47   Syncretism
- 49   Tom Ass Clarence
- 51   Citation
- 52   Reichstag 2
- 53   Art Against Art Not
- 63   Ancient Music
- 63   Getting Down!
- 64   The Heir of the Dog
- 65   Incriminating Negrographs
- 71   Bad People
- 72   The Under World
- 72   In The Funk World
- 73   Americana
- 73   Lowcoup

74	"Always Know"
75	History Is a Bitch
77	Size Places
79	To the Faust Negro to Sell His Soul to the Devil for That Much!
83	Black Reconstruction
87	In *The Fugitive*
88	Othello Jr.
93	Funk's Memory
95	Funk Lore
98	One Thursday I Found This in My Notebook
99	Duke's World
100	Afro American Talking Drum
102	Monk's World
104	Buddha Asked Monk
105	Monk Zen
106	Lullaby of Avon Ave.
107	The Dark Is Full of Tears
108	Fusion Recipe
109	JA ZZ : (The "Say What?") IS IS JA LIVES

for Amina

J. said, "Our whole universe is generated by a rhythm"

Is Dualism, the shadow inserted
for the northern trip. as the northern
trip. minstrels of the farther land,
the sun, in one place, ourselves, somewhere
else. The Universe
is the rhythm
there is no on looker, no outside
no other than the real, the universe
is rhythm, and whatever is only is as
swinging. All that is is funky, the bubbles
in the monsters brain, are hitting it too,
but the circles look like
swastikas, the square is thus
explained, but the nazis had dances, and even some of the
victims would tell you that.

There is no such thing as "our
universe", only degrees of the swinging, what
does not swing is nothing, and nothing swings
when it wants to. The desire alone is funky
and it is this heat Louis Armstrong scatted in.

What is not funky is psychological, metaphysical
is the religion of squares, pretending no one
is anywhere.

Everything gets hot, it is hot now, nothing cold exists
and cold, is the theoretical line the pretended boundary
where your eye and your hand disappear into desire.

Dualism is a quiet camp near the outer edge of the forest.
there the inmates worship money and violence. they are
learning right now to sing, let us join them for a moment
and listen. Do not laugh, whatever you do.

Masked Angel Costume

THE SAYINGS OF MANTAN MORELAND

Alabama

1. Never let a ghost
   Ketch you
         Never!

2. Avoid Death
     Ghosts
     Always
      be
       there!

3. Dead People
   & Live People
   Should not
   Mix!

4. Ghosts think they
      good lookin
   Never stay to find out!

5. I am mentioned in the credits
     but the ghost
       got the
         dough!

6 Cemeteries
   Funeral Parlors
   Morgues
   Do not need
   You while
   You
     alive

7 Never let Mr. Chan
 send you into
 a dark
  room
 by
   your self

8 If the dark get
  Noisy
  Seek
  light
   at
  Once!

9 Few people know
  my whole
   name.
    Nor
 if the name
  they call me
    is
    real.

10   Wait until
       the shooting
       stops
       then
       wait
       for
       witnesses
Leave as soon
       as it is
       safe.

11   I am a chauffeur
     when you see
        me
    But that is
      only
   in the
     movies.

12   I am never really
       laughing
     except
  off
  camera.

13   I made a lot of money
   & made people happy
     It was
     a job
   I accepted rather
      than
       preach
        or
      steal!

14   *Birmingham*
              Birmingham
was where
4 of my daughters
were killed

John Coltrane
composed
Alabama

It was the music
that moved
     my feet

          they never
     failed.

Sounding

A Measure, A Song, A Curse

And so the seasons, they tell us
are more important, than ourselves
flies and starlight, all the little
things. Except ourselves. Should you
want one, a self, any way. Detached
from the Death pile of this, the primitive
distortion, still. Prehistoric monsters
cave logic, uncooked stumblings, witchdoctoristic
shit. If you had a self
     If you was up under all that pile
     If you could still breathe or see
     beneath the assault of ancient deadly lies
     kept alive by the infinite sucking needles
     of rich white craziness, of schizophrenic negro
     craziness, the chauvinism of savages, disease
     for sale, famous rotting items to be eaten or
     smeared in the nose and ears, corpse parts
     to paste on the eyes, vomit music, which is
     quiet and stinks and full of vague balls
     flags made of twilight to wrap around anything
     sensitive until it smothers.
                                  (Head smashed through a door
                                    splinters jabbed in the neck
                                    blood is the number to ask for
                                    blind visionaries babbling)

They say everything is more important than a self. The whole
group of them. Stashed somewhere between the stars blinking
and blue, someone intelligent might find us, very very intelligent.
Wizards rattling gourds as your leg is about to drop off. A Muslim
appears, A Talmudist, A Christian, A Capitalist economist, the
rattling gets stronger and the leg finally drops off gangrenous
tootsie roll

No selves, only "eats" and "drinks" and drugs and "fucking". No
selves. What about only alone, there is no one else, its OK then,
no one can tell. A tree felled in the forest, there's no sound in
New York. It doesnt exist then, in Omaha or Heaven. No selves,
not together, thinking. Not alive and actually planning in the world
to change it. Not no science, no. No selves then, collected, and eyes
blinking. None of that. A coffin, lets kill ourselves. Lets get a bomb
a big explosive mushroom volcano and drop it on ourselves.
No selves. lets blow up everything. Lets blow up men and women
and children and thought and feeling. Lets make it flat and burned.
Lets be radioactive and write poems about paths in connecticut.
About birdbaths in vermont and wisps of smoke in south hampton.
no selves, not even one, except alone. an individual is OK, only
alone. not with touching and seeing in it. not with no intimate
whispering. Keep bullshit like love out of it. none of that. no selves.
only 12 hr barbaric killing of niggers and white ass working class
motherfuckers with hard hands.

Bees darting. A cloud. Light dancing. Twiddle dee and tweedle doo
and silent bumps. no being and stuff. no wanting except gold vinyl
spots. you can want gold vinyl spots. No being more, only being
less except you can be more if that is less. Or not real. or dies easy.
Or full of shit.

Just death. Call it open up and live. Call it mystery man. Music.
Call it hey hey hey eureka the freaka, say, ART! Let it rain fire but
it wont because it cdnt in the birdbath martini fingertip silences,
pages can be turned but have silly shit in em. quiet death.
Cheever in cold. in sides of stuff with no outsides. no connect.
no heat except from furnaces if you got oil. no warm – no warm –
no meaning. Ashes! Ashes! White people Academy Awards. Ashes!
Niggers in dinner jackets! Ashes. Fat nigger with comments.
Niggers with pulitzer prize cover story schizophrenia is OK. be a
indian. be anonymous. but dont be no indian like brown and off
somewhere hurting. be an indian if you aint an indian. if you really
an indian be something else. Ashes. Relics. Lets be relics,
but not too much of a relic. Not way back to black relics. no black
relics. vanished. lied. Stolen. Not like the shit the pope got hid in
his museum. something without blood. without sweat. without
words passing through ears. Ashes.

& no selves. Bombs are cool. Beatniks like bombs. Bombs are cool.
Ashes.

Death. Racism. Lies. Chauvinism. Oppression. Exploitation. Frustration. White movies. TV with only Nell Carter and the nigger midget.
And Benson. Fake families. Artificial. Be artificial. Be Oscar Wilde.
But dont try to fuck. Be cute. but no fucking. Stop fucking. Freaky
fucking is OK in a newspaper or rolled up in a window shade. or in
a book. No fucking. No babies. No real shit. No cold except cold as
nothing nothing out there. Ashes. Let bombs fall. Let killing be
everything then nothing. Conan the barbarian. Reagan the Conan.
Ashes. Fighting shd be over, peace. not peace where people are
happy. but peace of death. death peace. peace of death. silence and
ice death ashes. fire is over. traces of fire is OK but no fire in nothing. no heart of eye fire. no fire for food, except if cooked by silent

nigger, or laughing nigger, or different kinds of colored darkies who can be called names.

But no selves, hear? No breathing. No dancing. Except if you bounce. No rhythm. Either be on the wall or off the wall. But be against people having intelligence without degrees. No intelligence without degrees. Be for Norman Podhoretz dream of a world of ashes in which Reagan is crowned Lord God of Barbarians. Uphold Barbarians. Uphold Tarzan. Be Boy. Appoint Cheetah as Civil Rights Commissioner.
Uphold blackface but kill black faces. Darkies are great. Guys who can get along, and Gals. Uphold Gals. Pat em on the ass if it wiggles. Big ass Gals. And ashes. And bouncing. Be for bouncing. Bounce. And Death. Be for death. Death from the skies. Death as a result of barbarian economies. Greed Death. Stupid Death. Hail to Stupid Death & Bouncing. Hail to Awkward Dumb shit. And death. And sky death. And Gestapos and Nazis. Be for preachers who want to burn books. and Ashes. And bouncing. And death. No selves. No collections of them. Kill collections of selves. Alone is OK. solipsism. greed. individualism. and death. And ashes. And cold sand instead of warmth, or vibrance or rhythms, or intelligence loose in the world. Dead art. Art with feathers. Denying Art. Schizophrenic art. Ruler Art. Museum Art. No artists who want information or the world in it.

silence any art with the world in it or close to it or talking or thinking. kill light and heat that is among us. kill us. there is no us. only blindness and ice ages. no science. no love. no reason. no family. no communities of intelligence. no development. no loving human peace. Ashes. Stanley. Livingston. Sky death. No selves. dumbness. dull poems. bouncing. assassinations. klan sympathies. and ashes. and imperialist war. yes, that finally, and everything thing thing thing thing that supports or justifies it. stupid exclusive national chauvinism and R U (what))) and sidekicks and ashes and bouncing atomic war thats what we need atomic war we gonna get it theres no we, us i's is gonna, aint no us/es no no no only death and ashes and bouncing, no selves, fuck you kill you niggers, anythings, nothing but atomic death from rich people there is only ashes and bouncing thats all no love no selves no peace only atomic war and death and ashes thats all no no no self no no no no selves no no no no world no no no no no no no

Brother Okot
1931–1983

Our people say
death lives
    in the West
(Any one
 can see
    plainly, each evening
where the sun
goes to die)

      So Okot
      is now in the West

      Here w/ us
      in hell

I have heard
  his songs
    felt the earth
    drum his
    dance
his wide ness
& Sky self

      Ocoli Singer
      Ocoli Fighter

* *Okot P'Bitek, great Ugandan poet*

    Brother Okot
now here w/ us
in the place

Where even the Sun
    dies.

Forensic Report

The Killers cd wear
    spurs
    or
    medals

    Ears
cd be on
    their
    head

They cd be blonde
    & american
    & from the
    South

They cd speak American
    & live
    in Virginia
    or Maine
    or California
    or D.C.

They cd be wealthy
    & have a degree

They cd have little
    children
    who cd also

    be killers
    or have already
    killed

    They cd
    have proof
  that they killed
only out of necessity

They cd be dressed up
    or naked
    or both
    at once

They wd not have
    to laugh
    They could
    not have
    to love any thing

They could look
    perfectly
    normal
      to
    themselves

But be hated
    most places

They would not
    have to
    be seen
    drinking blood.

They wd not have to be known
    widely
      except
  as a metaphor

They wd not have to be sane
    They cd act crazy
    as well

They would not always
    be able
      to
        trick
      people.

    They cd
    be killed
in the right
    Situation

    IT'S
    NOT NECESSARY
    THAT THEY UNDERSTAND

    THIS.

Why It's Quiet in Some Churches

Just a Closeta Walk with Thee

Not a pin drops. No breathing. Please, please no sound.
("Make them niggers cut out that 'tom foolery'. Jesus,
ain't in Georgia!")
     You cannot make noise or the spirit will hear
     We'll nail up your mouth if you try to sing
     We changed the spelling of Prophet to Profit
     We changed Soul to Sole
     We covered spirit with a ghost
     We changed Sun to Son, and with the help of the right Farther
and knowledge of What Goest? He cd get his rightful inheritance.
No. we took the mother out. We burned broads from Salem to Troy.
From Soweto to Philadelphia to transform the pyramid of life
to a triangle of death. We took the head and nuts off the ankh
changed the life sign to a cemetery advertisement. Then had mfs
wear death around the necks they wd long for it so. We dis connected
creativity and art. But if it ain't no creativity ain't no art, and if ain't
no art even the schools must close, and the schoolmen go back to
Hairy Mystery!
The Father The Son And The Holy Ghost is a Joke
What happened to the Mother, Fools! There is no
life without the mortar and the pestle, the thing and
the thang, without boys and girls, women and men
in their blue quivering funk rising till jism
brings a new day.
We created tragedy by killing our fathers, fucking our mothers

putting out our own eyes, and wandering the world as an
                                   adverstisement for "modernism"
We separated thought from feeling. We thought feeling wd stop
us thinking, or vice versa. But then I do want to bore you.
And the cross roads we took recrossed, recrossed, and the
                                             cold north
was not that any more, but we were anyway, and then to exist
                                                 was only possible
w/ the slandered smoke of tortured change. From its we became ex-its!
We were signs but w/o the seed, blind, we had egos instead of eggs
the missing excitement, Gee, Baby, Sin! Our epitaph!

Sin Soars!

The American Peoples' Voice
    is never heard well
    is seldom heard
ABC CBS NBC Rocky Dupont Mellon Rich
    Thieves & Murderers is
    Pretend human real animals
    is Animal's that own network, newspaper
    chains, IBM, & them. Krupp
    & Dutch Phillips, the Japanese & German
    corporations, Israeli Bankers &
    the private collectors of the debt
    of any nation
    They
    is
    Not But Not
      the American
      people
their voice is never
        well seldom
        heard
English Department Skull & Crossbone
        New Critic Klansman is
        deconstructing the day
        name for night slaughter
        They laugh, They soul they do not have

    The American people voice
        Eurocentric Cultists
      of white supremacy own it
    they own the super structure
    for the business of planets
    shit namers
    we call them
    they name shit
    & get us to buy
    shit & eat shit
they voice is
they voice, is always,
        is
          heard

    But Not the American People
      not many people
        real people
        whole people

        Not Americans of any Kind – Definitely not
Native Americans or African Americans
                    Puerto Rican
                      or Chicano
              Americans
                      Central Americans
                      South Americans
    Invaders of Panama is
US/USSR Con artists ripping off Nicaragua
is, always is, Contras, Klan,
    Nazis is, Seldom the people
          is
The downside negative

But not the American people
the corporations censor the American
peoples' voice.
                       People who own
radio stations
                People who own
    tv networks
                  They can be heard
                  Chicken Kings
                  Hotel Queens

                  But not the American
people
    The American People
    Their voice
is never
    heard

So now they voices we hear are selling us
They voices carried in image profane
The voices & images jarring our favorite
    movies in shatters
        of sell

Like the German & Japanese Economies
They return via Dark Shadows
to Gold Light Hoorays
 Gold   Flood   Sun   Burst
       Hoo
         Rays

They sell CBS records & CBS
films, Miles & Monk & Billie
& Duke belong to Samarai ,Inc.
Frank Capra, Orson Welles, Sidney
Poitier, Rita Hayworth, belong
now to Samurai, Inc, a sub sidiary division of Standard
Oil of New York
  Gimme a S
  Gimme a O
  Gimme a N
  Gimme a Y

  S O N Y S O N Y
Standard Oil of New York

So they transfered control of German
& Japanese corporations at the end of
World War 2 to Rocky's holdings
Through Farben & Mitsubishi the good S
went on

With Marshall & his plan they lifted
the spoils, w/ our deaths & our toils
& gave them legally to themselves
While Truman lied & Eisen
hower choked on the oat meal.

They gave themselves money to defend
our wealth in their pockets as
security guards of Samurai, Inc.
As Samurai, Inc as Allah u
Akbar oil Gods, Inc., as legislators
governors, as money- & murder-dents

as any & every as what it is
was & their will over done

to the bone
to the minstrel grin
to the marrow of electrocution
to the splinters of serial kill
to the tap dances of thugs
        They cough up nothing but Germs
        In the ditch of history
        they lie
        They old & wiggle in ice cubes knocking
        Cold non rhythm jolt of
        Swastika
        the sauerkraut of
        vulture grease
        the hot dogs with
        black catch/up
        yellow retard
        omnipotent Frauds
        bounced help
    the money crosses water as dots
    & dashes smelling nothing
    the SOS is you breathing
    crossing the death row of
    Rockefeller's day dreaming teeth

they have sold our future to themselves
disguised as foreign languages
& dusty ledgers
the legs are sprawled so the dirty boots
elaborate the stillness

the letters awry
the tolls cooking us
the oil lamps of
brokeness
ghetto ness
Barrio Azul we
    clack
      maracas
      of the pulse
      the awaiting
as delusion cops a feel

Our map is not at all
      What it need &
         would be
           if we

      but then   our map
        is sliced out
        with the newspaper
        with the Morality
           of pay toilets
           & where we are
           is old business
        the blurred memory
           of certain
           arthritic dips

So why are we, the unheard, the ones
for whom democracy is a republican
        pornograph
          needing only a sharp slave
          to play

we the why do we who are burning
      our flags
      with the cocaine
      of them guys
      the propaganda fist
      of green backs
we who no have
      no see
      no know
    Why do we
Who are not with one person
      or
      one vote
      who went to electoral
      college
      to study
      Dip Craft
      Fraud Light
Who do not remember the 3 Musketeers
Who do not admit to being Dartagnan
Yet are
    from 1 second past
     monkey

why do we who are not heard
the American people
why do we not dig
      How come
        we dont under
            stand

That the US is Japan & Germany now
That Russia & China are the new Colored
Guys
     & the niggers are making all
       the trouble
     it's the niggers
     even they
     it's said
     are somewhere
     making trouble
& they doing, it's said, also
a good f - - - - - g
    job
  cause thats all
    we
    not
    knowing
     got

what news? no voice
        for the criminal
            class

you're just in time
    not to be.

No voice, insist our
     Not
     Masters
       the snake is
         rolling
        cross
        the
        ground

  Our saviour rolls across the clouds
in Air Force One   Is our voice
riding high w/ him?
       Heading for Panama, Nicaragua, Grenada

Now breathing vampire blood mixed
      w/ rat semen

     as he speeds
      toward Cuba
Atomic Enema Devil
Creator of Aids
Square hooligan with
     a Orange S

Where is our why
     our collection
     of questions
     that sizzle like
     beautiful black
     cartoon bombs

     But no one laughs
       at cartoons

They are like us who we are
    carriers
    holders
    receptacles
    vessels
    tools
flat money copping
    scribbles

Are you cripple?

Are you the people?

Does your church have a

  joke
  it tells
a long interesting payment
 of a story

there myth is welcome
  as green
   hills
 of Public School
  Mexico

that it was money, the articulate
  stuffing, and lives
  the history of flashes
    & gasps. Sudden shut metal
   doors

    & bullets whacking
   into the walls

Ode to the Creature

I didn't think this was
    the same jungle
    Bushman Bushman
    Nazi dream of Yale
    Bushman Bushman
    hung mouth of blood
    smeared to make eyes
    & mouth
      in the hood

    Bushman
    Bushman
You eat our skin &
      bones
    oh Bushman
      you

    I never wanted to be in Hell
      Yet here we is
      Bushman
      Bushman

    are you the devil
      or just *a* devil?

        I didn't care for this beating
              this crazed conversation
           of animal feces

Bushman Bushman
I have asked your picture
to be put on iodine labels

No one, Bushman
wd sleep w/ yr
    cheap greeting card
why haul the dead
        around

why not read the coroner's report

Yr dog is dead

  scribble scribble

X

    Everything we dont understand
        is explained
        in Art
        The Sun
          beats inside us
    The Spirit courses in and out
        of us

A circling transbluesency
    pumping Detroit Red inside, deep thru us
        like a Sea
                & who calls us bitter
                has bitten us
                    & from that wound
                        pours Malcolm
                                Little
                                by
                                Little

I Am

*for Addison Gayle, "The Black Aesthetic"
& Abdullah Buhaina*

Blues March

We are being told of the greatness
of Western Civilization
Yet Europe
is not the West

Leave England headed West
     you arrive
          in Newark,

The West is
The New World
          not Europe

The West is
     El Mundo Nuevo
     The Pan American
     Complexity
     As diverse as the routes
     & history
     of our collection

The West is The Americas
     not Europe

It is the America that the home
    boy tells, the sister we can
    see, yr wife, husband & children
  Yr mama
  Yr friends
  Yr family
  Yr closest enemies

      Are West, The quest
        The Search
        for Humanity
        still goes on

But of the Euro White Supremacists
    The Slave Masters
        Conquistadores
    Destroyers of Pharonic Egypt
          Carthage

    Invaders, Destroyers of Moorish Spain
        Of African and Asian Worlds
        Creators of the Inquisition
        Christ Killers
        Murderers of thousands of Christians
            in the Coliseum
        Murderers of Spartacus
           Vandals
           Germ Mens
           DitchMen
           Boers

Destroyers of Mohodarenjo
      Tenotchitlan
Killed Montezuma & Emiliano Zapata
Malcolm X, Martin Luther King, even
the Kennedies, Bobby Hutton, Fred Hampton
Medgar Evers,

    The Aztecs
    The Incas
    The Mayans
    The Taino
    The Arawak

Conquerors
   of
America

Enslaving

Humanity
  in
Cannibal
Menus

Bush men living on human
    flesh as public
    ritual
    ideology of predators
    & blood covered claws

Murderers of Iraq, wd be destroyers of
the ancient Mesopotamian culture

        Assassins of Sandino
        Toussaint Louverture, Patrice Lamumba

    Enslavers of Women
    Overthrew Mother Right
    Killed Socrates, Copernicus, Lincoln
    John Brown & Nat Turner
    Amilcar Cabral & David Sibeko

    Who claim Civilization & Christianity & Philosophy as
    Crucifiers who worshipped statues
        till 300 AD

    Who destroyed the libraries of Alexandria
        the University at Timbuctoo
    Who thought the wind made babies

Who say now they are the creators of Great Civilizations
    plagiarists, ignorant imitators
    claiming Geometry & the Lever

which existed 1000 years before
    they was even here
  whose great minds are thieves like
      Aristotle, Con men like
        Democritus & Anaximander
  whose Gods are the Vanilla Ice
      of Ethiopian Originals
     half dressed cave dwellers
      painted blue

Anglos (knife wielding) Saxons
    Sackers (Robbers) of Ancient Civilizations
Vikings whose Gods were drunk and rowdy
  robbers like Conan & Wodan

  Punks like Napoleon who
got run out of Haiti
   by Toussaint & Dessaline

    who got bum rushed out
      of Russia
    wacked out
    racist monsters
shot the nose & mouth
  off the Sphinx
  so sick &

anti-life & history were they
    who put Mali & Songhay &
    all Africa
    in Slave Ships

    for money, whose profits
were numbers not visionaries
Life as a low thing
worshippers of Mines not Minds
  War Lovers not Peace Makers

  Aint instead of Art
  (Death instead of Life)
     Dog they best friend
    Ice & Snow

    Not We & Know
    Blood Suckers &
        Mother Fuckers

Love War
so much
call the history
of their civilization

The Canon!

   in honor of Marco Polo's
    trip to China

Should we praise them
  for Dachau, for the poisoning
    of David Walker
    the Genocide of Native
     Americans
    or concentration camps
    for Japanese
     Americans

Perhaps 700 years of Irish Colonialism
   or Gandhi's
    murder
   The Conquest of India
   The Opium Wars
   TB Sheets for
   Indians
or the trail of Tears

So how should we praise them?
And what should we call them?
>	Who style themselves God
>	Whose New World Order
>	Seems old & Miltonian in that they rule
>	& do not serve

But somehow the term Satan seems too narrow
>	The word Devil is too limiting

But there must be some description, some appropriate horrific
>	we can coin –

>	Something that says liar, murderer, maniac, animal
>	something that indicates their importance.

Syncretism

    BAD NEWS SAY
    KILL
        DRUM
But Drum
no

    die

just
    act   slick

drum turn
 mouth
 tongue

      drum go voice
      be hand
      on over
        hauls
      dont die

      how some ever

drum turn slick

    never
    no drum
    never
    never
    die

    be a piano
       a fiddle
        a nigger tap
          fellah

      drum'll
        yodle
    if it need to

Thing say Kill drum
  but drum
      dont die/ dont even
           disappear

& drum cant die
    & wdn't

      no way!

Tom Ass Clarence

for Ol Black Joe

Ask these knees if there's
a negro attached
to them
Ask these knees
who they belong to
& how long they been here
pinned to the
        ground.

"These knees can talk, child!"
1st time I seen knees talk.
But these knees can talk
These knees can cry
These knees can even lie

Only knees had a program on tv
Only knees married to
      a pornography of naked nuns
Only knees can exist w/o anybody
      w/o no legs or thighs
            or feet or anything

Only knees can exist
            independent
            of anything
            completely
            by themselves
            autonomous

these are
Self made knees

prosperous knees
proud knees
shiny knees

These knees are
        Called
        Knee grows

                Like I sd
                These knees
                be on television
                They got they own
                      Show.

Citation

Now instead of Amos &
    Andy "integration"
   has given us
   The Skip & Spike
     Show
    Straight out of
    Pandora's Box

    Buttermilk covered
     Flies

    Come
    from the busted nut
    of square darkness

    Famous germs
    explaining diseased
    jism
    from the inside

Reichstag 2

How per fect that it was a Muslim
>Fundamentalist, one who shot Meir
Kahane (and was acquitted) the one
who was to be deported, one eyed
priest of an evil violent Muslim
cult. And it smells like Saddam or
The PLO, Quadaffi, Khomeini, the death threat
on Rushdie. Their hatred of Jews, their bloody
terrorism. And cheap greasy brown foreign
primitive violence.

The Mossad could do it, with the Serbs, cover the slaughter
>of Muslims in Bosnia. The Spook, Lee,
explained to niggers, for us, how Nigger
Muslims killed Malcolm. Farrakhan's
a Muslim. Elijah Muhammad. Malcolm
X was a Muslim.

It will be simple, like Americans,
>& greed will become
>>moral outrage.

Art Against Art Not

    Art Not is Devil Death
        Delusion
         like emptiness
          Silence
        the dark
        ignorance
    That everything that exists

        is alive

    Whatever there *wasiswill*
Space encompasses, yet the
    truth stares from it
      invisible as most
      of where we are

We are in the body of space
              as space
        in specific lives
           & waves

      Like foot prints breathing
        you'd have to
          Know

as you tune in with everything
possibility exists
alive

But space is filling
nurtures
the child

the sun

Where the history
thrusts as longing
withheld
gravity

bursts

the outcome

the meaning

inside the black hole

memory

grew
the 1st dick

to speak

Space
is speech

       the snake of Lightning
          Thunder clouds

Black snake the tongue of the world a blue
chord coming the milky way, the jizm
the stars shot out in. The electrical "Yes"
of livingness eternal as truth, beyond ourselves
yet in which we will always be part of however!
In that sudden sea of fire, memory becomes
consciousness, the fetus' tail becomes a solo
low & crawling across the earth, yet wise enough
to introduce the naked "people" to reality
& science. Even against the will of their
cruel invisible (land) Lord who told them that
      ignorance is obedience. Mystery is
Holiness. Expelled from paradise for listening
to the black talking snake, Dick Tongue, Blood is a see
song, the pen and the sword, Question & Answer.
The snake counciled the Whys & The Wise. Moving
like life itself, matter contradicted by motion
yet defining its existence & atom of universal
unity.

    The snake told the truth the invisible priest
hid knowledge to stay powerful. It was he who
brought the apple trees. Wasn't no Apple trees
in Africa before G got invisible & decreed the people be naked

too ignorant to live forever. And re enter inner
space closer to becoming again the consciousness of what
exists, Forever.

Spirit is created & continues through matter. The snake
carries the sun rising up & down, like
the heart beat, like lovers, waves of light
& see. The Snake whose name
begins with the same letter as the Sun, the twisting
rising breath of the world.

Blues
our favorite color
ultra violet
the soul is invisible
when it arrives
turning indigo
as it

  Grows visible
from the light
      of consciousness
      rising
      The Soul
is the Sun's
      History

it comes to understand
   life
    it's loss
    The Blown

  The Blowing

    The Blue

    Mother Sky

of the transparent

    Endlessness

      we blow

    The Blues

of sky & water

Wherein we wail

to bring forth the sea

the revelation of blow top

    Outness

to go into the

    Farther

    the way out
Trane blows all night

   Getting Happy

The Good News just above

The future is the lowest

heaven

comes

So it is the seeds wrapped in a bag

resembling infinity

the tallness

of the next

moment

When we were free

We were blue

but we blew

& became the blues

the beautiful sky & water

the sad song of the Sun

travelin

light

Because the Sun

    is Blue

& the world motor

    weres

      the engine

      is history

      Whirring

      in side

Yet Life became Money

    the Green Giant

    a television Star

    Gold at the Height

      orange

      at the Fall

      O.J.

      *

Understand the quest & the mystery.
That the circle, the whole is an entrance
a hole, a slit where from the old tongue
split by contradictions within, the dimension
& isness, what mothers, the me of am continuing
as so connected to everything by getting down
the blues lights the sky orgasm defines
little fish predicting Jesus coming
from inside the womb, the ego
of the earth traveling as mountains & breasts
pointing at the mother from the "gift", the
answer, yr question is a woman creating
the next is, the tale slipping out of the
exclamation of illusion from the mouth
of truth, everything from nothing, the new
like there is silence,
the last refinement
to speak as the sleep of electricity. The
whole, the all ways turns like a full moon
yet who can stare at the sun, the name
of what knew is the reality of "forever".

The snake was music the visible thought
the answer, as the Sea crawls in waves
the waves of is' story the shared center
What tells nature's needs the real u
the returning self following the soul
back to the right on, the mother
electric exploding measure as
a mirror, the wetness drenches
us with forever as a reflection

of the self's search for consciousness
we can become the matter of understanding
digging itself reexplain the history
of it's actuality, it's life, the
sign in the sky the unseen catching
a glimpse of it's Knowing, which being
is the self of it's will, the route
from which come comes, the forth
dimension which is motion, the on
switch, the self of everything as light
to see the egg on fire with vision
The body of Who, The Yes O Cean
which we leave when smart enough
to confuse naked people
that knowledge is sin

Be is the self twisting & rising & changing
the Beast is King, the body of is "visible" is
so the sea of gestation the waves of light
The I of the snake, history sings the self vision
to be a beast, the soul, anima, as the connector
of truth. What matter/is. Our mother – "life w/o
end", our father, the distance we are from
the creation of the world ourselves as perfect
& alive forever

    To be perfect is to be "invisible" forever
like the inside & outside of the circle. The
Snake lied & became the lion. The naked people
were put out of paradise for believing a snake.
The loins became cloth & sex
mysterious & dirty.

    The tree of Knowledge told them
nothing valuable. Like the Greek tortured
for stealing fire. Socrates poisoned. The Sphinx
sits fixed by her animal lower self. Her
visible self at the top is a woman
There is the soul of what creates, Alma
Mater, staring into the white invisible sky
human connected to no motion by an animal
the King of the Animals, crouching on his tale
headless as King, a powerful beast, who
cannot move disconnect from his eyes

Yesterday a comet fell into Jupiter from
the sky (at thousands of miles a second)
in massive fire balls of explosion
Sun Ra arrives

Ancient Music

The main thing
to be against
   is *Death*!

Everything Else
   is a
     Chump!

Getting Down!

Sisyphus explained
why he cant stand
Rock & Roll,

"The Judge sentence me to
the same thing
Then call these freaks
The Rollin Stones
To rub it in."

The Heir of the Dog

How amazed the crazed
 negro looked informed
 that Animal Rights had
 a bigger budget
 than the NAACP!

Incriminating Negrographs

Perceiving Miss

What do you think
of the movie
"X"?

Spike
Lie!

The Ho of Bup

"It was never about
yall. Hey, it was
always about
me

"Single negro on the
country club green
Only negro on the board
of International
Obscene

"Last name, Jackson
1st Name, Gunga Din

Hard shiny slave slobber
is whats left of
 my brain

"A Spike Lee Joint" Is A Negro Reefer

It makes believe
It gets you high.

"The Wages of Sin" Explained

Invoke the Nation
 to secure your fortune

Betray the Nation
 to receive your fortune

The X Is Black

(Spike Lie)

If the flag catch
    fire, & an x
    burn in, that x is Black
    & leaves an
    empty space. It
    is that place
    where we live
    the Afro American
    Nation

If the flag
    catch fire
    & a x burn in
    the only stripes is
    on our back
    the only star
    blown free
    in the northern sky
    no red but our
    blood, no white
    but slavers and Klux in hoods
    no blue
    but our songs

If the flag catch fire
    & an x
    burn in
    that x is black
    & the space that is left
    is our history
    now a mystery

we only live
where the flag
is not
where the air is funky
the music
hot
Inside the hole
in the American soul
that space, that place
empty of democracy
we live
inside the burned boundaries
of a wasted symbol
x humans, x slaves, unknown, incorrect
crossed out, multiplying the wealth of others

If the flag
    catch fire
    & an x burn in
    that x
    believe me,
    is black

Fresh Zombies

OK Shuffle. Stink in neon
Lie in lights. Betray before millions
Assassinate w/ slogans. Not old toms
but New Toms, Double Toms
A Tom Tom Macoute. Fresh Zombies
House Nigger maniacs. Oreo serial killers
That thumping, that horrible sound,
is not music, not drums, but shuffling
Not old toms, New Toms, Double toms
A Tom Tom Macoute. Fresh Zombies

Who Killed Malcolm X

The Same people who killed
    Kennedy
    & King
    & Bobby
    & Fred Hampton
    The same ones who
    shot Lumumba
    & Cabral. the same murderer
    cracker imperialism
who killed Bobby Hutton
    or Medgar Evers
    still directly connected

to the secret government
that killed Lincoln
that seceded
that had slaves
who locked Garvey up & deported him
who attacked & dishonored & lied about
    DuBois
        Who drove him
           to exile

Nat Turner & David Walker were killed
        by the same
        forces

The murderers of Vesey & Gabriel
Who destroyed Robeson
& humiliated Langston & Zora

Who killed
the little girls & blew up
that church
  in Birmingham

Who freed Emmett Till's
      murderers?
Who blew up Ralph Featherstone's
      car?

Bad People

We want to be happy
    neglecting
  to check
  the definition

We want to love
    & be loved
      but
      What does that
        mean?

Then you, backed up against
    yr real life

    claim you want
    only
    to be correct.

Imagine the jeers,
    the cat calls
    the universal dis

    such ignorance
    justifiably
    creates.

The Under World

Sd the Mayor
to the councilman,
"I never did respect
a preacher w/out a
church!"

Sd the councilman
to the Mayor,
"I never did respect
a queen w/out a
throne!"

In The Funk World

If Elvis Presley/ is
   King
Who is James Brown,
   God?

Americana

They hate the idea
of love, and disconnect
it from power and intellect
by claiming only 5 senses
& sex.

Lowcoup*

Craziness is no
    Act
        Not to
           Act

    is crazinezz

* Lowcoup is an Afro American verse form, as Haiku is Japanese!

"Always Know"
– MONK

If the animals
will not leave
of their own/ free
will

And Jesse Jump up
in a Donkey's tale
screaming "Let us Prey!"
Check it out

        He might not / even
        be talkin
        to you!

History Is a Bitch

Can you understand inside the cover you tell
    inside the problems the water falls on you
    it's not rain, there's no God so it's not "their"
    tears, nothing but thin air, in which the nigger
    bops like breath to be a ghost or a churl

I knew you when you didn't exist, a dead island where a few
    weirdos ran sheep. I laughed, the others too, explaining
    the icy fire that held it visible. Post card on
    the shore of a naked man and woman, the snake
    resembled yr mama.

We were a million years old by then & sleek with
    paraphenalia. Laid back under the trees for lunch
    casually noting the germs & their pitiful parrots

They smiled as we approached, like in a zoo with no attendants
    Don't think that twisting Blankness of dead caves
    didn't touch us. But drunk is laughing at it's best
    & the priests winked

Now it's thousands past, the moon & the sun don't even bother
    to appear. It's night they told us, *then*, & we didn't
    understand. oh boy, oh boy. Forget Christ & them

He never even got to Europe. It was a joke then, the
 Tarot spoke of the hanged man, & the
 imitation dancer wd immortalize
the fool.

Size Places

The unresolved future
The one dimensional delusion
like chauvinism is sickness
    HELL
        He Ill

        He Will

                Only He.

        2

it is an exactitude
how we live, forever, in Hells
    or Heavens

        3

The constancy
    of infinite motion
      into way

   Is we are our
only creators created
by our selves as we are
created by those in It that
created before

    4

   Beauty is
  More Beautiful
    we dig
than the
Ant Knows.

& Who
by that
Sees us as
tiny ignorant
   animals?

To the Faust Negro
to Sell His Soul to the Devil for That Much!

Oh Americans Who Have OverCome
Their Black Skin
But Are Still Sometimes
Confused w/ Afro Americans

Oh, Smart Negroes
Oh, Professional Over Standers
Oh, Sparkling Comfortable
Chattel, Slavemaster Condums
Poison Pus still oozing
from the living sores
of Plantation Leprosy

Oh. Bigtime LARGE LIVING
Corporate, Backward Buppie, Well Trained
Senior Playtoy Puppies, Negroes who have Made It/ Have Made
America Work For Them. Anti Afro American Charismatic Coons
Yo! Generals, Presidents, Deans, Chairs,
Yo! Medical Association Negroes, Tainted Mouthpieces,
Compradors, Quislings
Ubiquitous Rats, Fishy Public Officials, Shadow Sin Aiders
MayWhores, Media Pimps…
Dem Negro Crats, Reel Public Coons, Video Demons
    with Grant to act like Lee

        Ignorant History Distorting Ho's
        expensive important diamond studded
          Unisex Skeezers

Oh, glittering monsters blessed by The Supremist Lord
    of Imperial
    Whiteness

The Invisible god
    of
    Heathen
    Brain Fever
    Infection

Poison Fleas
    mashed throughout
    the
    falling
    Doo Doo

    plummeting
through the Colon
    Clarencing
    out the Ass

The Heathen "Word"
    for feces
    is
    Tom.

Drop out white behinds
with a low single splat
a fragment B
Flat
The Latest Hit
of Heathen Shit

Disappearing
covered with nasty papers
proving they had once been inside
The ADL's stomach

They spirit is the
BeezleBub
We Nose

Oh Ghosts of Rotten Past

Nice Negroes
reasonable about
    Slavery
armed with the Knee Pads
    of Their Class

    Kneeling
      to
     prey

    The Masters
    Answered
    prayers

Negro
Miracles
Created By The Power & Glory of Lies & Violence
Fraud & Force
By the bloody torture of his visible
Avatar the Heathen Cracker

Oh Niggers who love the very hatred of the whip
who sing like the blood cut out our hearts
Oh tap dancing, butt swinging, successful butchershop
mind stinking toilet paper lip well dressed wholly dishonest
souless paper academic flag pole living deformed mouth
woogies who lie through the caucasian chalk circle of their
constant giggle
who speak a language constructed from the masters farts

More and more I have come to believe
you will have to be eliminated
in order for the rest of us
to live.

Black Reconstruction

Oh Freedom segue to *Battle Hymn of the Republic*

      What the Doctor explained
         was that we had fought
         that we had patiently
         rushed into our trans
                      formed
      selves.

        That we had run away
from the plantations & closed
them down. That we had
plagued our liberators
to let us be liberated.
And offered our whole selves
as proof that God is real.
And we are his children.
And that there is a
Spirit in our suffering
that beats like twilight
red rain brown lit up
with thunder.
I cd see that then,
What that roar within us
the cymbals sharp &

glowing hot, as we put
on blue again, & became
ourselves, where we were,
as the angels in the chariot
ourselves, getting down to
make heaven our home.

That is the way it was told
When we put the Blue on
Again. With yes, the Blue
Steel bayonets, and the speech
of the prophets fashioned
out weapons of fire.

Then that rush, of a Gideon
Screaming madness high up
John Coltrane Savage Nigger
African Explosion Color

That the Freedom! The that
the yeh say what Bam!
Splat volcano language
of Free – Do you, The Free
The Bird – My sign, on my face
the skin raised, to show
out of fire, sky nut sperm
the jism that made the world
all the non stop lovely goodness
unstoppable screaming

It was like the ascension

itself, after 40 days
we were exploded into
the endless inspiration

To understand our lives
as they exist
              in the
              Spirit
              World

    the freedom of
    the always
    happy
    excitement
      of
      Love
       The Good
   The Living Laughter
      of all
        hearts

to be that as a world
as the creator
            of worlds

We knew we wd be saved
that it was in ourselves
our understanding
& acceptance
of our salvation.

But the redeemer
said he was covered
with blood. Of wolves
who tried to consume
the lamb
the black sheep
our souls, Ba Ba
our souls
are in our wool

& mine eyes
bear witness
to the Lord
& the glory of
his coming!

In *The Fugitive*

Richard Kemble kept insisting
he did not kill
his wife. That the real
murderer, was a one-armed
man.   He was telling the truth
all the time. And we knew it!
In the new series, if you watch
television, the real murderer
has become the Republican Senate Majority
Leader, who goes everywhere
with a pet lizard
who defecates through his mouth
& blows hot green gas out his tale.
Which, in certain conditions
oddly resembles low German.

Othello Jr.

(One Moor Time)

$

=

"

A Ne(gr)o Classical
Tragedy

of

"Amusement
& Contempt"

*

The Prologue

in

Three Lowcoup

I

AB, LHing on JEJ, Dig?

If James Earl Jones
    can play
    a Black Man

    The don't complain
    about Lawrence
    Olivier

    as
   O
Thell
   O,
             OJ?

II

Chris Darden

Othello & You
Othello Jr too
All worked for
The Christians

& like them Jigs
you got the old
gig. In the arena

as entertainment for
Barbarians

Surrounded
by all of em's
Lyins

& yr boy
O Jr
playing
Norman Bates

Making
  Faces
    &
      Screaming in Stares,

"You got my soul!
  I sold you my soul!

"I'll Kill to keep my Balls!

        III

If OJ is Othello
    Jr

& Vermin
is Iago

Marsha Clarke
Desdemona

& Cato
doofus Cassio

Johnny C.
The Man
who ran out
on his father

Chris
    the
        Arena's Prey

    Preying
    for Civilization

        Then
        Othello was Called
to go out & greet
        Hell
        & Fight
        for it.

    In love with
    Gold
    Enthralled by
    Otherness!

            But there is a
                Venice
              in California
          Where the Punic Wars
              Rage on

                & there
                 Moorish
                    Women
                     freed
                    his
                        Son!

Funk's Memory

Plays on & on place after place into futures past
It's passing It the is the is was been & going
Going is blowing gone is blown
Why the Funk remember
Why the Funk keep all we hearts

Like marching could be wind & noises
Like falling could be song
Like rising could be fire & lit skies
Like loving could be Music
never denied

All them to come was here when they left
    all us who left here is now
        about to come
            cause we in love
                what keep us breathing
                  is keep us a spirit
                    a point to pointing
                      a go to going
                        & we keep coming
                          Oh baby, is nightime
                            Joe Williams say nightime
                            is the right time

And it's like wind and cool blue &
 a life of pictures
 everything always
 alive.

Funk Lore

Blue Monk

We are the blues
    ourselves
    our favorite
     color
    Where we been, half here
              half gone

We are the blues
    our selves
    the actual
     Guineas
    the original
     Jews
    the 1st
     Caucasians

That's why we are the blues
    ourselves
    that's why we
    are the
    actual
     song

        So dark & tragic
        So old &
            Magic

      that's why we are
           the Blues
            our Selves

In tribes of 12
  bars
like the stripes
  of slavery
    on
  our flag
    of skin

We are the blues
    the past the gone
    the energy the
    cold the saw teeth
    hotness
    the smell above
    draining the wind
    through trees
    the blue
    leaves us
    black
    the earth
    the sun
    the slowly disappearing
    the fire pushing to become
    our hearts

& now black again we are the
whole of night
with sparkling eyes staring
down
like jets
    to push
    evenings
    ascension
    that's why we are the blues
    the train whistle
    the rumble across
    the invisible coming
    drumming and screaming
    that's why we are the
    blues
    & work & sing & leave
    tales & is with spirit
    that's why we are
        the blues
        black & alive
        & so we show our motion
            our breathing
            we moon
            reflected soul

    that's why our spirit
        make us

        the blues

    we is ourselves

        the blues

One Thursday I Found This in My Notebook

When love is perfected, when love
    is understood.
When love is the law
    & the measure
The ruler & ruled & body of
    of what is body mind of
what is mind
When love & the Soul
    are uncovered
then you will always
    sound like
        Duke Ellington.

Duke's World

Passion Flower
           for "Strays"

    is the explanation
    beauty makes
    the look of understanding
    a new day being so ancient
    brings

    There is an ascendance in Duke. A passage
through which you are pulled, where everything
that lives forever regards itself & lets you know
you can be there always when you are beautiful

There is no ugliness that describes Duke's world
        except what is not
        & how it connects to
        what is

It is not just the elegance, the irony, the
        sensuous self illumination
        there is also deep happiness
        in Duke's world

    What you think is a castle, expansive gardens
    is a teacher impeccably in love with
    exhaltation & joy. Duke's world
    is where we go if we are good.

Afro American Talking Drum

Duke

If you got real spooky
& became Duke Ellington
America wd deny it
just like they did
to the real Duke
Ellington

Ellingtonia

Duke
    speaks for everybody
& the Devil
    resents
        this!

It disturbed me
    so much

I was determined
    to ask him, the
        Devil,

Why this was
  So. Why did he resent

    Duke Ellington?

The Devil, not being a
    racist,
      explained

    (& in a very convincing
        way)

      that he didn't mind
        Duke
      it was his
        music
      that he
        despised!

Monk's World

'Round Midnight

    That street where midnight
    is round, the moon flat
    & blue, where fire engines solo
    & cats stand around & look
    is Monk's world

When I last saw him, turning around
    high from 78 RPM, growling
    a landscape of spaced funk

When I last spoke to him, coming out
    the Vanguard, he hipped me to
    my own secrets, like Nat
    he dug the numbers & letters
    blowing through the grass
    initials & invocations of the past

All the questions I asked Monk He
    answered first
    in a beret. Why was
    a high priest staring
    Why were the black keys
    signifying. And who was
    wrapped in common magic

   like a street empty of everything
   except weird birds

The last time Monk smiled I read
   the piano's diary. His fingers
   where he collected yr feelings
   The Bar he circled to underscore
   the anonymous laughter of smoke
   & posters.

Monk carried equations he danced at you.
What's happening?" We said, as he dipped &
   spun. "What's happening?"

"Everything. All the time.
   Every googoplex
   of a second."

Like a door, he opened, not disappearing
   but remaining a distant profile
   of intimate revelation.

Oh, man! Monk was digging Trane now
   w/o a chaser he drank himself
   in. & Trane reported from
   the 6th or 7th planet deep in

   the Theloniuscape.

Where fire engines screamed the blues
   & night had a shiny mouth
   & scatted flying things.

Buddha Asked Monk

"If you were always right
would it be Easier
or more Difficult
Living In The World?"

"I knew you'd ask that!"
Monk said, Blue and
Invisible.

Monk Zen

Monk
always
come in a
    place
later.
    Long after you first see
    him
    come in.

People say they
    didn't see him
    leave –

Miles say

    So What?

Monk say

    Well, You Needn't

Wilbur Ware say

    Me & Shadow & Trane was wit him when he went out
    You musta heard us!

Lullaby of Avon Ave.

I used to walk past Sassy's crib
a couple times a week, when young

And each time say, "That's
Where Sarah Vaughn lives".

That was when Symphony Sid
used to call her, "The Divine One",
Late nights, from hip Bird Land

Oh man, what a feeling that was
Divine & so hip & so very
beautiful.

The house is gone now
Symphony Sid too

As for the town, now
Sassy told us
just before she split

I'm gone, now
Send in

The
Clowns!

The Dark Is Full of Tears

    When Albert returned from
the grave, he had no horn. He
asked us to look for it &
we agreed.

    He sd he wd return when
we found it. He was somewhere
in space, drugged about Religion
& The Mob.

    I asked him had he been
murdered.

    "Of course", Albert wd answer
most things like this though,

    "Murdered by God! That's why
it was stupid to believe
in him!"

Fusion Recipe

Take a pinch of
   quote R & B

Add a smidgen/ of
   quote Jazz

Combine in a very shal
   low/ mildly heat
       ed/ Crock

  of "Uncle Sam" brand
        bovine fecal
          sauce

Then let the mixture sit
until it turns
   to
     cheap furniture.

JA ZZ : (The "Say What?")
IS IS   JA LIVES

Yes Bees !

God-Electric

Come Coming

Fire Jism

S H A N G O

CANTO JONDO

Eternity Power

Living Happiness

S P I R I T   L I F E

WORD SHIP

The Soul's Soul

SUN   THOUGHT   BREATH

Heart Beat

Is Going

Act Play

Ecstasy's   Now

Connecting   Endlessness

REAL   TRUE

LOVE   ALWAYS

SOUND   ARE

DIGGER   DIGGING

THE

WHO   BE

THE

WHAT   WATT

2

   Seer Seeing

SO   U   NeeDn't

   THE KEY
    of
   M O N K

M U N T U   K U N T U

  The Laughing South
     NIGHT'S MOTHER
  The Crying North
     DEY FATHER

   "Two Is One"

bottom to Top

 Hot to Cold

 new to Old

 See Navy

 Sea Crosser

 Trance Former

    Passing going

        The
    I   Am

    The Am Eye

      R
        B′
           ZZ

        The Silence of Sound

          The Power
          of Universal
           Orgasm

           The Sun's
            Nut
      The Thunder The Lightning

          The Two Hands

          The Dialectic

           WHO
           WHERE

       The You & I
        of Here & There

    THE DOWN UP

    THE BLUE MAN

        WHO

    THE WOMB MAN

    THE HUE MAN

        WHO

       Both
       Yall
        we
      I & I

        The
  US   IS

I am   Sings

   The Sun God
   Coming out
        His
        Mother

   The Ejaculator
   is The Ejaculation!

   Come Music!

                Visible Thought Herding

                 In Walked Dionysius

                    The Pyramid
                     change to
                 The Triangular Trade

                     The Spell
                     The Word

                     Good News
                     Hip Gnosis

                    Ghost Murder

                     Eat Mo
                 The Grain Crusher
                                        The Be er
                                                    The Alle
                     The Me
                      See

                   The See Me
                   The Me Sea
                      Waves

 NIGHT BLUE
     DAZE
  THE DERE DAT

   The Eye
      On

          The
                DEATH DEAD!

          The Living Knowing

                THE
                STAY GO

              CHURCH   SPEECH

              The STING
              Of
                    NIGGER PRINTS

                  MOON'S SON

                      YOU
                        I

            The So
                &
            The So

            The Where

                the
            were so

         the
      Sower

      Gravity
      The Meaning

         the
         GO
         How

      The blue
                  blown
            The Blues
                  what we blew

                  Hawk Honk
                  Black Bird Aflame

                  The smile rising
                  the changes the circle
                        the hole

                  The Whole

                  The Hard Empty

                  The upside down
                  the twist to
                  frown

The cold circle checker
The hot opposite the cross the water, before whatnot

the dooji
the vonhz

other stuff
flying anyway

the chord you came in on

The To Where
    The Every
        The body of joy

          The Why

          The Or

          Elgeba's Cymbal

          The Y he show you
          Yes, The Cross Roads

              G's Us
             the stiff joint
              The hot poem
              Volcano balls
              The planets humming

           The head circle
           the lost ankh
           The Resurrection
     What John Said
           Revelations

           We are alive
           We are humans
           ruled by heathens

     Trying to Remember the formula
                         for killing ghosts

           The underground
                dark blue speed
                     star checking

     black freedom lady
           the kiss of light

                     the orchestra sky
                        comet language

           africamemorywhisper

                     blowing
                  the blown the known
                          what we knew

                    what we blew
                    blues loves us
            our spirit is ultraviolet

            what we knew
            drumwhich

            the long measure
            my man
                    treehip
                    her son

Becoming the One

LITTORAL BOOKS

Norma Cole, *My Bird Book* (1991)
Paul Vangelisti, *Villa* (1991)
Pasquale Verdicchio, *Isthmus* (1991)
Fanny Howe, *The End* (1992)
Martha Ronk & Don Suggs, *Desert Geometries* (1992)
Douglas Messerli, *Along Without* (1993)
Douglas Messerli, *The Walls Come True* (1995)
Amiri Baraka, *Funk Lore* (1996)
Stephen Ratcliffe, *Sculpture* (1996)